# Aliyah –
# God's Last
# Great Act of
# Redemption

## Dr Richard F. Gottier

## Sovereign World

Sovereign World Ltd
PO Box 777
Tonbridge
Kent TN11 0ZS
England

ISBN 1 85240 308 X

Typeset by CRB Associates, Norfolk, United Kingdom
Printed in the United States of America.

# Contents

|            | Foreword                                | 5  |
| Chapter 1  | *Aliyah* and the Sweep of Scripture     | 9  |
| Chapter 2  | The Foundation of Holiness              | 17 |
| Chapter 3  | The Land: To be Treated as Holy         | 29 |
| Chapter 4  | Or the Land Will Spew You Out           | 39 |
| Chapter 5  | Diaspora: God's Ultimate Judgment       | 47 |
| Chapter 6  | *Aliyah*: God's Final Redemptive Act    | 53 |
| Chapter 7  | *Aliyah*: God Reclaims the Land         | 61 |
| Chapter 8  | *Aliyah*: God Redeems the Chosen        | 73 |
| Chapter 9  | *Aliyah*: God Restores the Covenant     | 81 |
| Chapter 10 | *Aliyah*: God's Refining Fire           | 89 |

# Foreword

This book grows out of three intensely personal encounters with the Lord, as well as a compelling word from the Holy Spirit that this message must be written. Each of these encounters would profoundly change my life and my ultimate relationship with *aliyah* – God's ingathering of the Jewish people to Israel.

The first of these crucial events stretches back nearly three decades. I had known God's call to teach His Word since earliest childhood, but nevertheless had gone through a very liberal graduate education and drifted dangerously close to humanism. On January 15, 1974, with deep hunger in my heart, I returned unconditionally to my Lord. At the heart of this return was a new affirmation of the authority of God's Word.

Over the ensuing months my heavenly Father sovereignly rearranged my schedule at the university, allowing me to spend four to six hours a day in His Word. For an entire year the Holy Spirit led me to just two subjects: my own need for a renewed mind, and the place of the land of Israel in Old Testament teaching. For months, the Lord spoke of the place of the land in His covenant with Israel, how He directed her in claiming the land, and the holiness which His land demanded from its inhabitants.

Over the years God led me back to the subject of the land and the covenant many times. Ultimately, we taught our own Good Shepherd Fellowship for eighteen months on the land as the prototype of the Lord's calling on each of us, and as the covenant foundation for our church.

As a result of a longstanding friendship with Gustav and Elsa Scheller, founders of the Ebenezer Emergency Fund ministry, we were drawn into God's call on their lives to open a holy highway into the far reaches of the 'land of the north' – Russia – in order that His scattered chosen people might flow home. In fact, we were so deeply involved with Ebenezer that I began to see a real danger that my primary call to teach God's end-time remnant might slip through my hands.

Some four years ago I earnestly sought the Lord on this matter, and His clear response was the second confirmation of the primacy of the land in my life. As the Holy Spirit led me to a familiar promise from my earlier call, in Isaiah chapter 49, He again assured me that His Word would be a sharp sword in teaching. Now, however, He urged me to read on. His call also included bringing *'Jacob back to Him, in order that Israel might be gathered to Him'* (Isaiah 49:1–5). Somehow I knew that He would reveal to me how the teaching of His Word to the remnant is inextricably bound up with His holy work of gathering home His chosen people.

The third holy encounter came only a few weeks ago. By now I had searched the prophetic scriptures about aliyah and had taught widely on God's purposes and the Ebenezer ministry. Yet, on an afternoon in mid-June, I stepped into our bedroom to pick up an item.

Suddenly the Lord began to speak of *aliyah* with such marked clarity and intensity that I dropped to a bench at the foot of the bed to listen. For perhaps an hour and a half He poured the light of His Spirit onto the return, the covenant and the land. I had previously understood that, through the ingathering of Israel, He was fulfilling His covenant promise never to abandon His chosen people in a strange land. But now the Lord began to explain that not only is *aliyah* holy, but that through *aliyah* He is accomplishing His last great act of redemption. For Israel's sake, and for His covenant, He will use *aliyah* to cleanse the land and restore its prophetic borders. Through *aliyah*, the Father will put a new heart in His chosen people and confirm a new covenant simultaneously. Yet *aliyah* is more – it is our God's last offer of redemption to the nations! And His last call to the church to come through the refining fire to her first love.

In writing, I have made two conscious decisions. I have tried to keep a potentially exhaustive text quite compact in the hope that, with greater brevity, a much wider audience would read and understand. This of necessity has set limits on the number of scriptures cited, frequently leaving dozens out. I trust these decisions are the proper ones, and that as a result God's purposes in restoring the land will be more readily grasped.

As you read, I pray that much of the 'mystery' surrounding end-times prophecy will be clarified, and that many apparently unrelated events we see occurring at this time will be 'fit together' into the final picture of His plan.

# Chapter 1

# *Aliyah* and
# the Sweep of Scripture

Around the world today a miracle of monumental proportions is taking place, as God restores the ancient land that He chose in covenant with Abraham, and gathers His people to Himself from all over the world. So great is this miracle that more than one million people have been gathered back to the land in the decade beginning in 1991. Yet, as I travel around the nations, I find that few have any real understanding of the place that Israel plays in the economy of God in these closing moments of history. Further, *aliyah* is viewed by some as a rather exotic idea. As I was sharing the joys of my own heart over *aliyah*, one pastor commented: 'I suppose if God has burdened you for it, that is fine; but it is certainly not for everyone.'

I propose to you that *aliyah* is not simply an exotic idea. Rather, Israel, the land, and the ingathering of the Jewish people are God's last great witness to the nations that He is still the God of heaven and in control of all history. A multitude of scriptures bear witness to our heavenly Father's heart for this day, as Isaiah summarizes:

*'Do not fear, for I am with you; I will bring your offspring from the east, and gather you from the west. I will say to the north, "Give them up!" And to the south, "Do not hold them back." Bring My sons from afar, and My daughters from the ends of the earth.'*
(Isaiah 43:5–6)

While the word *aliyah* sounds strange to our ears, it was common in Semitic languages, including biblical Hebrew. Very simply, *aliyah* meant 'to go up, to ascend'; 'to go from to a lower place to a higher place'. Gradually, *aliyah* became associated with the journey of Hebrew families three times a year up to Jerusalem and the Temple Mount, there to celebrate the three great festivals which the Lord had commanded. Psalms were written to accompany this joyous occasion. Fathers led their families up the highway to Jerusalem, to the feast, singing the psalms of *aliyah*. Even today your Bible may indicate that some of the psalms are called psalms of ascent, to be sung as people ascended to worship in Jerusalem.

Over the centuries, this returning to Jerusalem for the feast days came to be associated with the restoration of a man's soul to his God. In the midst of great praise and worship and the reading of Scripture, the need for contrition, repentance and renewed obedience was again clear. Consequently, as men associated the restoration of their souls and spiritual life with the ascent up to the Temple, the whole concept of *aliyah* came to mean a return, almost in the sense of revival in contemporary usage.

Now, as the Word of God unfolds before our very eyes, and the Lord is seen to be gathering His children from the remote parts of the world, the concept of *aliyah* becomes natural to describe all that is involved in returning to the land. Out of this has come its generic use. It is in this comprehensive, generic sense that I use the word throughout this book, and in this meaning we shall discover God's last great act of redemption.

However, before we can see *aliyah* sketched out in full, we must first grasp the biblical concepts and the ways of the Lord against which this final return is portrayed. The Word of God is ever of one piece. His ways with Abraham and Moses are still His principles today. Jesus said, *'I came not to destroy the law, but to fulfill it.'* In other words, 'I did not come to change the rules of the kingdom of God, but to make it possible for you to obey them.'

Put very simply, the whole of Scripture is an account of God's mercies and redemption as He draws man back to Himself again and again through great redemptive acts. Only the first three chapters of Genesis stand apart from this picture. These opening chapters unveil three profoundly crucial matters in the economy of God's kingdom. First, the majesty of our Lord's **creation** as He unfurls the heavens and the earth. Second, we see God's **purposes** unfolded as He creates man in His own image and gives him reign over His creation. The Eternal Father intended to fellowship with this created being, who would walk in obedience and righteousness before Him. Yet, third, hardly does their fellowship begin, when man listens to the enemy of God and **rebels against his Maker** by eating from the tree of knowledge of good and evil.

By this treachery man not only sins against God, but in high treason barters away to Satan his divinely appointed dominion over creation. Most tragic of all, man forfeited his high privilege that was at the heart of

11

creation – his access to the heart of God – and their fellowship is severed, seemingly forever.

All the Word of God following Genesis chapter 3 is an account of the Lord's love for man and His tender mercies, offering redemption to willful and rebellious hearts. While the tender hand of the Father reached down to many men in their personal need for redemption and forgiveness, I find only four times in Scripture where the Father addressed redemption on a massive, worldwide basis.

By the sixth chapter of Genesis, the corrupt seed that was within the heart of Adam had birthed a people so godless, so wicked, that the Lord Himself would say that the wickedness of man was great on the earth, and that *'every intent of the thoughts of his heart was only evil continually'* (Genesis 6:5). Another translation says, *'Every imagination of his thoughts was constantly evil.'* The Lord gave man 120 years to repent, and instructed a God-fearing man, Noah, to build a great ark for those who would believe the Word of God and escape the coming flood. A fallen race would be renewed through the seed of a godly man.

Yet, hardly had the ark rested on Ararat when the seed of Noah again rebelled. Men of Shinar were now building a tower that would reach unto heaven and challenge God Himself. The Lord confuses their language and scatters them abroad, and the stage is set for His second great act of redemption.

In this corrupt land of Shinar, Babel and Ur, the hand of God touches another God-fearing man – Abram. From Genesis chapter 12 through the end of Malachi, the thirty-nine books of the Old Testament present a detailed account of God's dealings with Abram and his seed, and His preparation for the coming Redeemer. At the heart of God's dealing with Abram (whom He renamed Abraham, 'father of a multitude') was the covenant of promise, bringing man into eternal relationship again with his Creator God. This eternal, unbreakable covenant pledged God's perfect protection, provision and blessings in return for the obedience of Abraham and his seed to the statutes of God. Two thousand years of Israel's vacillation between rebellion and repentance, and God's response of both judgment and blessing, comprise the thirty-nine books of the Old Covenant.

Here is the supremely crucial factor: interspersed with our Lord's dealings with the men and women of the Old Covenant, and their willful stubbornness, are flashes of hope and mercy. There are pledges from prophetic vision that God has promised never to reject His chosen people utterly and finally. The Holy Spirit injects dozens of promises of final restoration and redemption. And, perhaps most hopeful, these promises are dated 'in that day' or 'in the last days', pointing directly to these closing hours of history.

If we understand that God's ways, His standards and His Word are eternally true, then we have a major clue to understanding the Lord's heart and His ways of dealing with His chosen people in these last days. To understand fully God's dealings with Israel through the Old Covenant, we must first appreciate His call and His love for His **chosen people**, His irreversible **covenant** with them, and the awesome purity of **the land** as the object of this covenant. If we can comprehend the centrality of these three concepts on the basis of the Old Covenant Scriptures, then we may be quite certain that He will deal in like fashion in the redemption of His people today.

## A chosen people!

In keeping with His eternal plan, the Father looked for a man or a family, a people with whom He could fellowship in holy purity, and whose worship would spring out of a righteous heart. Such a people would be a powerful demonstration to the nations that our God is a Holy God, and that He can be trusted to keep covenant. As Isaiah would say many years later, Israel was to be *'a light to the nations'* (Isaiah 49:6) *'and a people after God's own heart'*.

## A righteous covenant!

The essential nature of God as revealed in every age is that He is a God of His Word, and that He looks after His Word to keep and to perform it. No fewer than eight times God spoke to Abraham about keeping His covenant and His Word. In Genesis chapter 15 we have a picture of the actual cutting of the covenant. Scholars tell us that there were at least eleven steps to the cutting of a covenant, but the essential point is that such a covenant was utterly unbreakable. So we have a righteous God who called a God-fearing man who believes in His Word. With him, God has cut a covenant that is inviolable, unassailable.

## A holy land!

A covenant, however, must have an object. Should you and I agree to sell real estate, I might offer you my home for $100,000 and you might agree that that is a fair amount to pay for it. The object of our agreement, our covenant relationship, is that you will place in my hands a check for $100,000 and I will place in yours the deed to the property. But the object throughout is the property – the land.

I believe that the most misunderstood concept in the entire Old Testament is the concept of the land. Hebrew scholars tell us that the land – *eretz* – occurs in the Old Testament more than twenty-five hundred times. So central was the concept that we can never understand Old Testament Israel, nor Israel today, without understanding the land. Note the opening eight verses of Exodus chapter 6. As God spoke to and through Moses, He summarized all three of these concepts:

> 'Then the LORD said to Moses, "Now you shall see what I will do to Pharaoh; for under compulsion he shall let them go, and under compulsion he shall drive them out of his land." God spoke further to Moses and said to him, "I am the LORD; and I appeared to Abraham, Isaac, and Jacob, as God Almighty, but by My name, LORD, I did not make Myself known to them. And **I also established My covenant with them, to give them the land of Canaan,** the land in which they sojourned. And furthermore I have heard the groaning of the sons of Israel, because the Egyptians are holding them in bondage; and I have remembered My covenant. Say, therefore, to the sons of Israel, 'I am the LORD, and I will bring you out from under the burdens of the Egyptians, and I will deliver you from their bondage. **I will also redeem you with an outstretched arm and with great judgments.** Then I will take you for My people, and I will be your God; and you shall know that I am the LORD your God, who brought you out from under the burdens of the Egyptians. And I will bring you to the land which I swore to give to Abraham, Isaac, and Jacob, and I will give it to you for a possession; I am the LORD.' " '
> (Exodus 6:1–8)

The Lord says He has appeared to Abraham, Isaac and Jacob as God Almighty; that He also established His **covenant** with them to give them the **land** in which they sojourned; and that He has remembered His **covenant** and will **redeem** them with outstretched arm and with great judgment. They will be His **people**, and they shall know that He is the Lord their God. He will bring them to the **land** which He swore to give to Abraham.

A chosen people, a righteous covenant, a cleansed land. On these three foundation stones God built Old Testament Israel. And if we would comprehend all that He is doing in redeeming His people today, we would do well to understand all that His Word promises on these matters for these last days. With our unchangeable God, His covenant promise of forever is still forever. The prophetic borders of the land still stretch from the great river to the great sea. His mercies and redemption are still true.

# Chapter 2

# The Foundation of Holiness

The focus of this book is the awesome act of redemption which our God is carrying out right before our very eyes. It is the agenda that occupies His heart in these last moments of history. Yet, if we are to understand His redemption and restoration, we must have a clear picture of His original plan for His people. From the beginning, He intended to have a holy people, who would keep righteous covenant while dwelling in a purified land. God's desire was always to fulfill His original, creative purpose, and have a people of such purity and obedience that He, the sovereign God, could walk in fellowship with them.

That brief phrase in Genesis 3: *'They heard the sound of the Lord God walking in the garden in the cool of the day,'* is but a momentary glimpse of all that the Father desired for His created children. Before Adam's great act of treachery and treason, the Father God could walk in the midst and find no sinfulness of heart on the part of man to offend His pure heart. From the Lord's call of Abram out of Ur, through His restoration of the nation of Israel under Moses, every command was designed to bring about a people of such purity and holiness that He could dwell among them.

## A holy people!

As Moses penned the words of the law, we find him returning to this subject again and again:

> *'Do not render your souls detestable through any of the swarming things that swarm; and you shall not make yourselves unclean with them so that you become unclean. For I am the Lord your God. **Consecrate yourselves therefore, and be holy for I am holy** ... For I am the Lord who brought you up from the land of Egypt to be your God; **thus you shall be holy, for I am holy.'*** (Leviticus 11:43–45)

Always, by illustration, the Lord was drawing the line for Israel between the sacred and the profane, the pure and the impure, the clean and the unclean. Again Moses wrote:

> *'Then the Lord spoke to Moses, saying, speak to all the congregation of the sons of Israel and say to them, **"you shall be holy, for I the Lord your God am holy**. Every one of you shall reverence his mother and his father, and you shall keep my sabbaths; I am the Lord your God. Do not turn to idols, or make for yourselves molten gods; I am the Lord your God."'* (Leviticus 19:1–4)

The standard of holiness is clearly the Lord Himself; the eternal plumb-line is His nature and His Word:

> *'You are therefore to make a distinction between the clean animal and the unclean, and between the unclean bird and the clean; and you shall not make yourselves detestable by animal or by bird or by*

*anything that creeps on the ground, which I have separated for you as unclean.* **Thus you are to be holy to Me, for I the Lord am holy; and I have set you apart from the peoples to be Mine.'**
(Leviticus 20:25–26)

*'The Lord will establish you as a holy people to Himself, as He swore to you, if you will keep the commandments of the Lord your God, and walk in His ways. So all the people's of the earth shall see that you are called by the name of the Lord; and they shall be afraid of you.'* (Deuteronomy 28:9–10)

God promises to establish Israel as a holy people among the nations, even as Isaiah would proclaim, *'A light to the nations'* (Isaiah 49:6). Again Moses writes:

*'And you shall be to me a kingdom of priests, and a holy nation.'* (Exodus 19:6)

**Holy? Holiness?** The Hebrew root means quite simply, 'pure, devoted, dedicated'. There follow the derived meanings of separated – separated from and separated to. Through Adam's fall, sin has come into the world. A holy people must be separated from that sin and separated to a Holy God. In the Torah, this concept of holiness is repeatedly shown to be equivalent to obedience to divine command, paying reverence and heeding the Word of God. The book of Deuteronomy is replete with illustrations:

*'Now this is the commandment, the statutes and the judgments which the Lord your God has commanded me to teach you,* **that you might do them in the land** *where you are going over to possess it, so that*

19

*you and your son and your grandson might fear the Lord your God, to keep all his statutes and His commandments, which I am commanding you, all the days of your life, and that your days may be prolonged.'* (Deuteronomy 6:1–2)

*'All the commandments that I am commanding you today **you shall be careful to do**.'*
(Deuteronomy 8:1)

*'You shall therefore love the Lord your God, and always **keep** His charge, His statutes, His ordinances, and His commandments.'* (Deuteronomy 11:1)

*'These are the statutes and judgments that you shall **carefully observe** in the land which the Lord, the God of your Fathers, has given you to possess, as long as you live on the earth.'* (Deuteronomy 12:1)

Further on in Deuteronomy these commands for holy obedience become associated with the promised blessings of God, and disobedience is linked with the judgment of God:

*'Now it shall be, if you will diligently obey the Lord your God, **being careful to do** all His command-ments that I command you today, the Lord your God will set you high above all the nations.'*
(Deuteronomy 28:1)

Here, then, is the Lord's foundation for His second great act of redemption through Abraham's seed. A holy people set apart from the world and from sin, so that the sovereign God of heaven might fellowship with them; that they might be a holy people and a light to the nations.

*'The Lord will establish you **as a holy people to Himself**, as He swore to you if you will keep the commandments of the Lord your God, and walk in His ways. So all the peoples of the earth shall see that you are called by the name of the Lord; and they shall be afraid of you.'* (Deuteronomy 28:9–10)

## A holy covenant!

How intricately the people and the covenant are intertwined in the heart of God and in His Word. The holiness which God desires and commanded of them was to be measured by their obedience to the covenant He had made with their father Abraham. Through the covenant the Lord spelled out His expectation of the chosen people, and through the covenant He pledged to Israel His unswerving protection and provision forever. At least eight times God spoke to Abraham to reveal the nature and scope of His covenant with him and his seed forever. Note this classic example:

*'Now when Abram was ninety-nine years old, the Lord appeared to Abram and said to him, "I am God Almighty; walk before me, and be blameless. And I will establish My covenant between Me and you, and I will multiply you exceedingly." And Abram fell on his face, and God talked with him, saying, "As for Me, **behold, My covenant is with you**, and you shall be the father of a multitude of nations. No longer shall your name be called Abram, but your name shall be Abraham; for I will make you the father of a multitude of nations. And I will make you exceedingly fruitful, and I will make nations of you, and kings*

*shall come forth from you.* **And I will establish My covenant between Me and you and your descendants after you** *throughout their generations* **for an everlasting covenant, to be God to you and to your descendants after you.** *And I will give to you and to your descendants after you,* **the land of your sojournings, all the land of Canaan, for an everlasting possession;** *and I will be their God." God said further to Abraham, "now as for you, you shall keep My covenant, you and your descendants after you throughout their generations. This is My covenant, which you shall keep, between Me and you and your descendants after you: every male among you shall be circumcised."'* (Genesis 17:1–10)

But how shall we understand the nature of a covenant? The following verses give an indication of the covenant God cut with Abraham:

*'And He said to him, "I am the LORD who brought you out of Ur of the Chaldeans, to give you this land to possess it." And he said, "O Lord GOD, how may I know that I shall possess it?" So He said to him, "Bring Me a three year old heifer, and a three year old female goat, and a three year old ram, and a turtledove, and a young pigeon." Then he brought all these to Him and cut them in two, and laid each half opposite the other; but he did not cut the birds. And it came about when the sun had set, that it was very dark, and behold, there appeared a smoking oven and a flaming torch which passed between these pieces. On that day the LORD made a covenant with Abram, saying, "To your descendants I have given this land, from the river of Egypt as far as the great river, the river Euphrates."'* (Genesis 15:7–10, 17–18)

An exhaustive discussion of covenants is beyond the scope of this text, but an earthly covenant could be cut between any two men who wanted to make a solemn vow to each other concerning a matter of extreme consequences. Most common would be a covenant of mutual protection between kings, as in that between Abraham and the kings of the valley in Genesis chapter 14. There were at least eleven steps in the cutting of the covenant. Briefly, the two men would slaughter a large animal and lay out the two halves. Then, as they walked in a figure eight between those halves, they would repeat the vows delineating the extent of their commitment to each other. All the while they were pointing to the slaughtered animal and saying, 'may God do so to me and more so if I do not keep the words of this covenant.'

The essence of the covenant was the utter unthinkableness of ever breaking it for any reason. So complete was this commitment to covenant vows, that if one partner tried to break them quietly, undetected, and thereby betray the covenant, his own family would turn him over to his covenant partner, and he would pay with his life for that betrayal. It is this sanctity of covenant vows that lies behind the many hundreds of Old Testament references to Israel's covenant with God. By way of illustration, the Scriptures portray our own marriage vows as covenant vows, and therein we see the measure of the sacred vows that husband and wives take with each other. We also see the eternal consequences of the casual way in which modern man treats those vows.

Perhaps the most clarion warning of how sacredly the Lord holds His covenant agreements with Israel can be found in the cry of the prophets. Isaiah summarizes it succinctly:

> '*The earth will be completely laid waste and com-pletely despoiled, for the* LORD *has spoken this word. The earth mourns and withers, the world fades and withers, the exalted of the people of the earth fade away. The earth is also polluted by its inhabitants, for they transgressed laws, violated statutes, **broke the everlasting covenant.***'
> (Isaiah 24:3–5)

And from Jeremiah:

> '*The word which came to Jeremiah from the* LORD, *saying, "Hear the words of this covenant, and speak to the men of Judah and to the inhabitants of Jerusalem; and say to them, Thus says the* LORD, *the God of Israel, '**Cursed is the man who does not heed the words of this covenant** ... They have turned back to the iniquities of their ancestors who refused to hear My words, and they have gone after other gods to serve them; the house of Israel and the house of Judah **have broken My covenant which I made with their fathers.**' Therefore thus says the* LORD, *'Behold I am bringing disaster on them which they will not be able to escape; though they will cry to Me, yet I will not listen to them.'"*'
> (Jeremiah 11:1–3, 10–11)

We can almost hear the words of the Jewish leaders to Jesus as they cried out, 'We have Abraham as our father'. In effect, they were arguing that their covenant was with Abraham, and that God would never break His covenant with them. Yet their statement sidestepped the heart of the covenant vows: by their very rebellious behavior they could void the covenant. Ezekiel speaks of this:

24

*'And you shall say to the rebellious ones, to the house of Israel, "Thus says the Lord God, Enough of all your abominations, O house of Israel, when you brought in foreigners, uncircumcised in heart and uncircumcised in flesh, to be in My sanctuary to profane it, even My house, when you offered My food, the fat and the blood; for they made My covenant void – this in addition to all your abominations."'*

(Ezekiel 44:6–7)

As Daniel describes the monstrous king who will rule the world in these closing hours of history, the most damning thing he can say of this king is that he shows favor to those who *'forsake the holy covenant'* (Daniel 11:30).

A holy people called into an eternal relationship with God by a holy covenant. This relationship is based on the very foundation of faithful obedience to the heavenly Father. From an unchangeable God who never changes either His requirements or His promised blessings, we can begin to grasp the outline for Israel's final return today. God's great final act of redemption – *aliyah!*

## A holy land!

A holy people and a holy covenant. But a holy land? I believe that the concept of a pure land is the key that unlocks our understanding of God's last great act of redemption. A holy God made a covenant with His people which demanded righteous living. But remember, every covenant has an object. It might be the mutual agreement between two kings to protect each other should a stronger nation attack either of them. Or a vow of mutual provision in the midst of famine.

25

Or, in our own terms, the piece of real estate which we agree to transfer from one to another for a given sum of money. And in the great unfolding drama of God reaching out to His people in redemption, the land of Israel is clearly the focus of His holy covenant.

In our Lord's first words of His call to Abram, He said, *'go forth from your country . . . to the land which I will show you, and I will make you a great nation and I will bless you . . . '* (Genesis 12:1–2). As Abram journeyed from Ur through Haran, he came to Canaan and passed through the land to Shechem. Here God appeared again to him and said, *'To your descendants I will give this land'* (Genesis 12:7). Note carefully that the promise of the land came even before the covenant. In God's first two revelations to Abram He mentioned the land twice, with a direct commitment that the land would be his:

> *'Now the* LORD *said to Abram, "Go forth from your country, and from your relatives and from your father's house, **to the land which I will show you;** And I will make you a great nation, and I will bless you, and make your name great; and so you shall be a blessing; And I will bless those who bless you, and the one who curses you I will curse. And in you all the families of the earth shall be blessed." So Abram went forth as the* LORD *had spoken to him; and Lot went with him. Now Abram was seventy-five years old when he departed from Haran. And Abram took Sarai his wife and Lot his nephew, and all their possessions which they had accumulated, and the persons which they had acquired in Haran, and they set out for the land of Canaan; thus they came to the land of Canaan. And Abram passed through the land as far as the site of Shechem, to the oak of Moreh. Now the Canaanite was then in the land. And the*

LORD *appeared to Abram and said, "To your descendants I will give this land." So he built an altar there to the* LORD *who had appeared to him.'*
(Genesis 12:1–7)

All this before the covenant promises! At Bethel, the herdsman of Abram and Lot began to quarrel over lack of pasture. They resolved their differences, with Lot choosing the plains of the valley and Abraham settling in the land of Canaan. It was here that God gave His most profound promise to Abram, again before the covenant:

'*And the* LORD *said to Abram, after Lot had separated from him, "Now lift up your eyes and look from the place where you are, northward and south-ward and eastward and westward; for* **all the land which you see, I will give it to you and to your descendants forever.** *And I will make your descend-ants as the dust of the earth; so that if anyone can number the dust of the earth, then your descendants can also be numbered. Arise,* **walk about the land** *through its length and breadth;* **for I will give it to you.**" *Then Abram moved his tent and came and dwelt by the oaks of Mamre, which are in Hebron, and there he built an altar to the* LORD*.'*
(Genesis13:14–18)

After nearly three decades of searching the Scriptures concerning the land, I stand today in wonder and awe at the majesty with which our heavenly Father speaks of that little piece of middle-eastern real estate. Anything close to a comprehensive survey of all that the Word says about the land would be the making of many books. Thirty-eight of the thirty-nine Old

Testament books speak of the land. Over twenty-five hundred times the land (*eretz*) is mentioned. So central is it to the thesis of this book that I must devote several pages to its understanding.

# Chapter 3

# The Land: To be Treated as Holy

The Hebrew mind divided its understanding of the land into two distinct concepts. First, there was the land as tillable soil, *adamah*, the ground from which life springs. From my own boyhood days on a farm in the American Midwest, the *adamah* is a most pleasant picture. In the long hours of discing and preparing the soil for planting, I would frequently scoop up a handful of that fine, rich dirt and let it trickle through my fingers. It was from this *adamah* that our Lord formed the first man, and it was from the *adamah* that He named him Adam.

The second Hebrew concept, *eretz*, included the soil, but much more. It embraced the fields, the mountains, the valleys, the rivers and streams, the trees, the rocks; and the sweep of the land into the distance to clearly defined borders. And yet there was so much more – there was a clear sense of belonging, of intimacy; of the Jewish people belonging to the land and the land of Israel belonging to them. There is an old American folk song: 'This land is your land, this land is my land.' Not long ago Carol and I drove by those same fields where I spent many hours as a boy with horses and tractor. Dad and Mom have gone to glory, and as I paused before those fields, I realized that the record of deeds in the county courthouse now says that our name is upon the land. Although our recognition of that ownership is transitory, and it will be passed on to another at our going to glory, we felt a sense of belonging as we looked across those fields that 'this land is our land'.

For Israel the **land**, *eretz*, was all of this and yet infinitely more. The Eternal God, Creator of the Universe, had said to Israel's father, Abraham:

> *'Lift up your eyes and look from the place where you are, northward, and southward and eastward and westward; for **all the land which you see**, I will give it to you and to your descendants **forever**.'*
> (Genesis 13:14–15)

**Forever!** There is no terminus, no cut-off date to the covenant promises made by the very God of heaven. Forever! Think of it: a deed to the land recorded in heaven has for 4,000 years read **'belonging to Israel'**. I may be but a *goy* – a gentile – to Israel, but I have arrived in that land many, many times by ship and by plane. To this very day I cannot set foot on the tarmac of Ben Gurion or Haifa, but a lump comes to my throat, and a tear to my eye, as I look up and say, 'Father, this is truly Your land'.

This brings us to a central point. Any land to which God has laid claim is holy, and anyone entrusted with that land must treat it as such. Through Moses, God gave detailed instructions on how to claim the land, and how to conserve it and retain it forever. The problem was that the land had been occupied for a very long while by pagan people who worshiped false gods and idols. Their thoughts and deeds were utterly reprehensible to a holy God. **The land must be**

**purified**, sanctified and kept clean in recognition of its heavenly owner.

Note just a few of God's many instructions through Moses for purifying the land:

> *'Hear, O Israel! You are crossing over the Jordan today to go in to dispossess nations greater and mightier than you, great cities fortified to heaven, a people great and tall, the sons of the Anakim, whom you know and of whom you have heard it said "Who can stand before the sons of Anak?" Know therefore today that it is the LORD your God who is crossing over before you as a consuming fire. He will destroy them and He will subdue them before you,* **so that you may drive them out and destroy them quickly,** *just as the LORD has spoken to you. Do not say in your heart when the LORD your God has driven them out before you, "Because of my righteousness the LORD has brought me in to possess this land," but it is because of the wickedness of these nations that the LORD is dispossessing them before you.'*
>
> (Deuteronomy 9:1–4)

> *'For if you are careful to keep all this commandment which I am commanding you, to do it, to love the LORD your God, to walk in all His ways and hold fast to Him;* **then the LORD will drive out all these nations from before you,** *and you will dispossess nations greater and mightier than you. Every place on which the sole of your foot shall tread shall be yours; your border shall be from the wilderness to Lebanon, and from the river, the river Euphrates, as far as the western sea. There shall no man be able to stand before you; the LORD your God shall lay the dread of you and the fear of you on all the land on which you*

31

set foot, as He has spoken to you. *"See, I am setting before you today a blessing and a curse: the blessing, if you listen to the commandments of the* LORD *your God, which I am commanding you today; and the curse, if you do not listen to the commandments of the* LORD *your God, but turn aside from the way which I am commanding you today, by following other gods which you have not known."'*

(Deuteronomy 11:22–28)

And in a third passage:

'*These are the statutes and the judgments which you shall carefully observe in the land which the* LORD, *the God of your fathers, has given you to possess as long as you live on the earth. You shall **utterly destroy all the places** where the nations whom you shall dispossess **serve their gods,** on the high mountains and on the hills and under every green tree. And you shall tear down their altars and smash their sacred pillars and burn their asherim with fire, and you shall cut down the engraved images of their gods, and you shall obliterate their name from that place. You shall not act like this toward the* LORD *your God. But you shall seek the* LORD *at the place which the* LORD *your God shall choose from all your tribes, to establish His name there for His dwelling, and there you shall come.'* (Deuteronomy 12:1–5)

A central principle of the Word of God is that the Lord's awesome holiness will brook neither compromise nor mixture. Few men can be tempted outright to deny God, or will openly rebel against Him and His commands. Yet many who profess God's name can be drawn subtly into compromising His ways, or be

32

tempted to add mixture to the pure Word of God. Against this background, Moses issued repeated warnings:

> *'I will be an enemy to your enemies and an adversary to your adversaries ... You shall not worship their gods, nor serve them, nor do according to their deeds; but you shall utterly overthrow them, and break their sacred pillars in pieces. **You shall make no covenant with them or with their gods.** They shall not live in your land, lest they make you sin against Me; for if you serve their gods, it will surely be a snare to you.'* (Exodus 23:22, 24, 32–33)

The focus of this word is that a holy people dares make no covenant with an unregenerate world. Any compromise with the idol worshippers already in the land will undermine the very resolve that it takes to drive them utterly out of the land, as God commands. Failure at this very point explains much of the failure of Israel throughout the Old Testament period. As the tiny remnant returned from the Babylonian diaspora, and under Ezra's godly leadership the people listened intently to the reading of the Scripture, their first point of repentance was that they had mixed and inter-married with the people of the land. These words ring through the Torah: make no covenants with the people of the land, drive them all out utterly:

> *'Watch yourself that you make no covenant with the inhabitants of the land into which you are going, lest it become a snare in your midst. But rather, you are to tear down their altars and smash their sacred pillars and cut down their asherim for you shall not worship any other god, for the LORD, whose name is Jealous, is*

*a jealous God – lest you make a covenant with the inhabitants of the land and they play the harlot with their gods...'* (Exodus 34:12–15)

In fact, in the book of Numbers God's warning becomes so intense that He even pledges to do to Israel what He would have them do to other people if they did not obey:

*'Then you shall drive out all the inhabitants of the land from before you ... but if you do not drive out the inhabitants of the land from before you, then it shall come about that those whom you let remain of them will become as pricks in your eyes and as thorns in your sides, and they shall trouble you in the land in which you live. And it shall come about that as I plan to do to them, so I will do to you.'* (Numbers 33:52, 55–56)

In another warning:

*'When you enter the land which the* LORD *your God gives you, you shall not learn to imitate the detestable things of those nations. There shall not be found among you anyone who makes his son or his daughter pass through the fire, one who uses divination, one who practices witchcraft, or one who interprets omens, or a sorcerer, or one who casts a spell, or a medium, or a spiritist, or one who calls up the dead. For whoever does these things is detestable to the* LORD; *and because of these detestable things the* LORD *your God will drive them out before you. You shall be blameless before the* LORD *your God.'* (Deuteronomy 18:9–13)

The final outcome on the slippery slope of compromise and mixture with the pagan people was that they would ultimately lead the children of Israel into the occult, and even Satan worship.

We have seen that the land, granted unto Abraham by a divine pledge, was his as he walked out his faith across it step by step – *'every place on which your foot shall tread'*. Under Moses, the Lord adds this additional requisite: for a holy people to serve a holy God under the terms of a holy covenant, the land bearing God's name must also be holy. Therefore that land must be swept clean of the peoples whose lives and worship were an abomination to God. So unequivocal was this command that they were even forbidden to have any dealings with, or cut any covenants with, these pagan nations. There must be no room for the temptation to compromise with evil, and thereby open the door to the temptation to serve their idols and take their daughters as wives.

Perhaps the most striking example of God's intent to have a pure land is found in Deuteronomy chapter 21. The very simple principle is that there must be expiation for every sin; the people must be free of guilt; and the land must be washed clean of every taint. The illustration here covers the case in which no one can be found who is accountable for a murder. What is to be done to maintain the holiness and integrity of the land?

*'If a slain person is found lying in the open country in the land which the LORD your God gives you to possess, and it is not known who has struck him, then your elders and your judges shall go out and measure the distance to the cities which are around the slain one. And it shall be that the city which is nearest to the slain man, that is, the elders of that city, shall take a heifer of the herd, which has not been worked and*

35

> *which has not pulled in a yoke; and the elders of that city shall bring the heifer down to a valley with running water, which has not been plowed or sown, and shall break the heifer's neck there in the valley ... And all the elders of that city which is nearest to the slain man shall wash their hands over the heifer whose neck was broken in the valley; and they shall answer and say, "Our hands have not shed this blood, nor did our eyes see it. Forgive Thy people Israel whom Thou hast redeemed, O LORD, and do not place the guilt of innocent blood in the midst of Thy people Israel. And the blood guiltiness shall be forgiven them. **So you shall remove the guilt of innocent blood from your midst**, when you do what is right in the eyes of the LORD."'*
>
> (Deuteronomy 21:1–4, 6–9)

✓  Our contemporary minds have been so clouded by secular humanism that we have difficulty grasping the purity that a holy God demands. Humanism touts the highest good of all as not love, but tolerance. No judgmental claims of guilt may be lodged against any man's sins. This so colors our thinking that we can hardly understand the biblical sacrifice that is made for expiation for the sin of murder, when no one present is apparently guilty.

Perhaps no word in all Scripture is so pointed on this matter as that given to Moses in Exodus chapter 33. While the great prophetic leader tarried before God on the holy mountain, the people induced Aaron to make a pagan idol in the form of a golden calf. As Moses discovers the awfulness of the sin they have committed, he returns before the Lord and pleads for their forgiveness and their lives, even offering his own life as pledge. The Lord's response:

36

*'Then the* LORD *spoke to Moses, "Depart, go up from here, you and the people whom you have brought up from the land of Egypt, to the land of which I swore to Abraham, Isaac, and Jacob, saying, To your descendants I will give it. And I will send an angel before you and I will drive out the Canaanite, the Amorite, the Hittite, the Perizzite, the Hivite and the Jebusite. Go up to a land flowing with milk and honey; for I will not go up in your midst, because you are an obstinate people, **lest I destroy you on the way."** . . . For the* LORD *had said to Moses, "Say to the sons of Israel, You are an obstinate people; should I go up in your midst for one moment, **I would destroy you . . . "'***

(Exodus 33:1–3, 5)

Long before they came to the sacred land, the people had so grieved their Lord that He finally determined that no one over the age of twenty would be allowed to enter the holy land. His awesome word was: *'Lest I destroy you on the way,'* and again: *'I would destroy you.'* I know of no other word in all scriptures which so poignantly identifies man's problem in the presence of a holy God. Small-minded men cynically mock a Holy God by saying that He has simply composed a set of rules to see if man will obey them. In fact, the matter is far more severe because, apart from God's infinite mercy and forgiveness, His very presence and holiness would consume us as sinful men and women.

However, let us not lose our focus. A holy God called to Abraham for a holy people to live before the nations as a light to the world, as evidence that a people can live holy lives before their God. The Lord confirmed this call on His people through a covenant made with Abraham, Isaac and Jacob and renewed through Moses, that this people should live righteously before Him on the land He had designated. This land, by its very nature because chosen by God, is holy. Consequently, the land demands to be treated righteously by those called by God to live on it.

I personally believe, with some confidence, that as we observe God carrying out His final act of redemption, His first step will be the renewing of the purity and righteousness of the land. Even as I write, I believe that we can clearly see the hand of God bringing about the steps that will cleanse the land.

# Chapter 4

# Or the Land
# Will Spew You Out

Both Jesus and Paul spoke of our being entrusted with the mysteries of the kingdom of God, so let us pause to examine one of the most awesome of these mysteries. People will sometimes say of Israel, 'But it is just real estate; how can it be holy?' Yet so intimately was the Father's heart intertwined with the hearts of His chosen people, and so profound was the covenant that bound them together, that only a holy people could abide in the fellowship of a holy God. From God's earliest words to Abraham, the land was both the object of these covenant promises and its greatest reward.

A land whose borders were repeatedly defined, and to which the eternal God has affixed His name, is by definition holy. Here the Lord would not only place His Name, but He would dwell among His people and receive their worship. So sacred was this trust of the land, that the truth of the its purity came bubbling up in the midst of Moses' prophetic instruction. In Leviticus he is rehearsing a long list of moral sins which Israel must avoid at all costs, and suddenly he cries out:

*'You are therefore to keep all My statutes and all My ordinances and do them, so that the land to which I am bringing you to live will not spew you out. Moreover, you shall not follow the customs of the nation which I shall drive out before you, for they did all these things, and therefore I have abhorred them. Hence I have said to you, "You are to possess their land, and I Myself will give it to you to possess it, a land flowing with milk and honey. I am the LORD your God, who has separated you from the peoples."'*

(Leviticus 20:22–24)

What a wealth of meaning the land connotes for Israel! With every step they took they were reminded that they were in covenant relationship with God and enjoyed His protection. He had told Israel that they would not need to build walls or hedges or fences, but that He Himself would be their strong protection. As long as they obeyed Him, they need fear no enemy attack. The land was a constant promise of His provision and His blessings – truly a land flowing with milk and honey. Again under the covenant, the land was their pledge of eternal possession, not only for them but for their children's children and for generations afar off. And the land was cause for great rejoicing, as they lifted their worship and joyful singing on the great feast days. Oh, the pain, when in Babylon they finally realized what they had lost:

*'By the rivers of Babylon, there we sat down and wept, when we remembered Zion. Upon the willows in the midst of it we hung our harps. For there our captors demanded of us songs, and our tormentors mirth, saying "Sing us one of the songs of Zion." How can we sing the LORD's song in a foreign land? If I forget*

*you, O Jerusalem, may my right hand forget her skill. May my tongue cleave to the roof of my mouth, if I do not remember you, if I do not exalt Jerusalem above my chief joy.'* (Psalm 137:1–6)

As the inseparable bond between people and land comes into focus, we can almost feel the prophet Jeremiah cringe as he sees the defilement of the land. Jeremiah surely wept as he spoke for the Lord:

*'For My eyes are on all their ways; they are not hidden from My face, nor is their iniquity concealed from My eyes. And I will first doubly repay their iniquity and their sin, because* **they have polluted My land***; they have filled My inheritance with the carcasses of their detestable idols and with their abominations.'*
(Jeremiah 16:17–18)

*'... *  **Why is the land ruined***, laid waste like a desert, so that no one passes through? And the* LORD *said, "Because they have forsaken My law which I set before them, and have not obeyed My voice nor walked according to it, but have walked after the stubbornness of their heart and after the Baals, as their fathers taught them," therefore thus says the* LORD *of hosts, the God of Israel, "behold, I will feed them, this people, with wormwood and give them poisoned water to drink."'* (Jeremiah 9:12–15)

Again Jeremiah envisions **the land in mourning** because of the awfulness of the sin committed in it.

*'As for the prophets: My heart is broken within me, all my bones tremble; I have become like a drunken man, even like a man overcome with wine, because of the*

41

L ORD *and because of His holy words. For the land is*
*full of adulterers; for the land mourns because of the*
*curse. The pastures of the wilderness have dried up.*
*Their course also is evil, and their might is not right.*
*"For both prophet and priest are polluted; even in My*
*house I have found their wickedness," declares the*
L ORD *.'* (Jeremiah 23:9–11)

From Ezekiel, perhaps most graphic of all:

*'Then the word of the* L ORD *came to me saying, "Son*
*of man, when the house of Israel was living in their*
**own land, they defiled it by their ways and their**
**deeds;** *their way before Me was like the uncleanness*
*of a woman in her impurity. Therefore, I poured out*
*My wrath on them for the blood which they had shed*
*on the land, because they had defiled it with their*
*idols."'* (Ezekiel 36:16–18)

The warning of the prophets sounded as a clarion call
to Israel again and again; yet the remedy was simple
enough that even a child could obey. One of God's
central promises through Moses was that of long life on
the land. They would not be cast off, but would rather
live in the great joy of the covenant promises. The
Torah is replete with such reminders:

*'So you shall not wrong one another, but you shall fear*
*your God; for I am the* L ORD *your God. You shall thus*
*observe My statutes, and keep My judgments, so as to*
*carry them out,* **that you may live securely on the**
**land.** *Then the land will yield its produce, so that you*
*can eat your fill and live securely on it.'*
(Leviticus 25:17–19)

To live securely on the land! Provision, blessing, protection and peace – all were a certain promise of the Father if they would but follow their covenant commitments:

> *'You shall not make for yourselves idols, nor shall you set up for yourselves an image or a sacred pillar, nor shall you place a figured stone in your land to bow down to it; for I am the LORD your God. You shall keep My sabbaths and reverence My sanctuary; I am the LORD. If you walk in My statutes and keep My commandments so as to carry them out, then I shall give you rains in their season, so that the land will yield its produce and the trees of the field will bear their fruit. Indeed, your threshing will last for you until grape gathering, and grape gathering will last until sowing time. You will thus eat your food to the full and live securely in your land. I shall also grant peace in the land, so that you may lie down with no one making you tremble. I shall also eliminate harmful beasts from the land, and no sword will pass through your land.'* (Leviticus 26:1–6)

It is arresting to note that even as God gave the Ten Commandments to Moses, only one of them carried a promised blessing:

> *'Honor your father and your mother, that **your days may be prolonged in the land** which the LORD your God gives you.'* (Exodus 20:12)

Some may argue that this applies only to personal longevity, but I would suggest that, in the context of God's repeated emphasis upon the land, a submissive heart and an obedient spirit would assure a pure land

and many generations on it. (Just as the foundation of this promise is respect and honor for one's parents and for authority, conversely, one of Satan's major weapons of destruction in our contemporary society is to promote rebellion of children against their parents. We should hardly be amazed that our land is polluted!) This recurring plea for humble obedience is reconfirmed in Moses' valedictory words:

> *'So you shall observe to do just as the* LORD *your God has commanded you; you shall not turn aside to the right or to the left. You shall walk in all the way which the* LORD *your God has commanded you, that you may live, and that it may be well with you, and **that you may prolong your days in the land** which you shall possess.'*          (Deuteronomy 5:32–33)

He reaffirms the promise:

> *'You shall therefore keep every commandment which I am commanding you today, so that you may be strong and go in and possess the land into which you are about to cross to possess it; so **that you may prolong your days on the land** which the* LORD *swore to your fathers to give to them and to their descendants, a land flowing with milk and honey.'*
> (Deuteronomy 11:8–9)

We now come to a point of stunning realization. As a God of righteousness seeks to draw His chosen people into a place of righteousness, He makes the measure of that holiness their day by day walk on the covenant land. Sanctified by the Father's name and His presence, this land becomes holy even as the Father is holy. Inanimate creation responds to the Creator's presence, and in purity would spew out a rebellious people. The land, potentially one of God's greatest blessings to Israel, can thus at the same time be her greatest judgment. Jesus said that even the rocks would cry out in praise if the children were quiet that first Palm Sunday. Here the land, sanctified by the Father, carries the potential for judging Israel as she walks upon it. When the mercies and grace of a tender heavenly Father are tested to the limits, there is finally a time of judgment:

> 'Do not defile yourselves by any of these things; for by all these the nations which I am casting out before you have become defiled. For the land has become defiled, therefore I have visited its punishment upon it, **so the land has spewed out its inhabitants**. But as for you, you are to keep My statutes and My judgments, and shall not do any of these abominations, neither the native, nor the alien who sojourns among you for the men of the land who have been before you have done all these abominations, and the land has become defiled; **so that the land may not spew you out**, should you defile it, as it has spewed out the nation which has been before you. For whoever does any of these abominations, those persons who do so shall be cut off from among their people.'
>
> (Leviticus 18:24–29)

One can almost hear Paul crying out to the Romans:

> 'For since the creation of the world His invisible attributes, His eternal power and divine nature, have been clearly seen, being understood through what has been made, so that they are without excuse.'
>
> (Romans 1:20)

45

God's very creation is adequate witness to any man of his need of the gospel. So Moses prophesies: be obedient to all God demands of you, or the very land, pure and in league with its Creator, **'will spew you out.'** What a background for understanding the diaspora of the Jews, and what a foundation for the present *aliyah*.

# Chapter 5

# Diaspora:
# God's Ultimate Judgment

This book purposes by its title to be about *aliyah*. By now many of you may wonder if we have lost our way. The answer is clearly, not at all. *Aliyah* is about the ingathering of God's chosen people – the ingathering of God's chosen people back to their land – but this people and the land are so inextricably bound up together that we can never hope to understand the people apart from the land, or the land apart from the people. We come, then, to one of the most pivotal questions in this discussion: if the people are not on the land today, what happened? Why must they be gathered back again? The Lord's purposes for Israel are captured succinctly in Psalm 37:

> *'Trust in the Lord, and do good; dwell in the land and cultivate faithfulness. Delight yourself in the Lord; and He will give you the desires of your heart ... Wait for the Lord, and keep His way, and He will exalt you to inherit the land ... '* (Psalm 37:3–4, 34)

However, the God who knows our hearts so intimately and how treacherous they are, made full provision and gave clear warning to Israel if they did not keep His commandments in the new land. There is a summary of God's forewarned judgment in Leviticus 26:14–33. Before we examine excerpts from this critical passage, note that the Lord always begins with the gentlest judgments on us, and the judgments cease when we turn in repentance back to obedience to Him. Yet as Israel steadfastly and stubbornly refused to be obedient, the judgments escalated steadily, until the final judgment in every prophetic account is that God would scatter them from the land:

> *'But if you do not obey Me and do not carry out all these commandments, if, instead, you reject My statutes, and if your soul abhors My ordinances so as not to carry out all My commandments, and so **break My covenant**, I, in turn, will do this to you: I will appoint over you a sudden terror, consumption and fever that shall waste away the eyes and cause the soul to pine away; also, you shall sow your seed uselessly, for your enemies shall eat it up. And I will set My face against you so that you shall be struck down before your enemies; and those who hate you shall rule over you, and you shall flee when no one is pursuing you. If also after these things, you do not obey Me, then I will punish you seven times more for your sins. And I will also break down your pride of power; I will also make your sky like iron and your earth like bronze. And your strength shall be spent uselessly, for your land shall not yield its produce and the trees of the land shall not yield their fruit. If then, you act with hostility against Me and are unwilling to obey Me, I will increase the plague on you seven times according to your sins. And I will let loose among you the beasts of the field, which shall bereave you of your children*

*and destroy your cattle and reduce your number so
that your roads lie deserted.'* (Leviticus 26:14–22)

In striking crescendo the judgments of God increase,
each seven times more intense than the last, until the
final judgment:

*'I will lay waste your cities as well, and will make your
sanctuaries desolate; and I will not smell your sooth-
ing aromas. And **I will make the land desolate** so
that your enemies who settle in it shall be appalled
over it. **You, however, I will scatter among the
nations** and will draw out a sword after you, as your
land becomes desolate and your cities become waste.'*
(Leviticus 26:31–33)

Can it really be that, worse than wars and famine
and wild beasts, is to be disenfranchised from the
land? Ah, yes! To be torn from the covering of God's
protection; torn from His loving provisions; torn from
His presence and the joyous worship at the great feast
days – and then, worst of all, to be torn from the tender
hope that the land of God's covenant promise was
beneath their feet. Moses, in his great valedictory on
the east side of the river Jordan, spoke these foreboding
words:

*'So watch yourselves, **lest you forget the covenant** of
the LORD your God, which He made with you, and
make for yourselves a graven image in the form of
anything against which the LORD your God has
commanded you. For the LORD your God is a consum-
ing fire, a jealous God. When you become the father of
children and children's children and have remained
long in the land, and act corruptly, and make an idol*

*in the form of anything, and do that which is evil in the sight of the* LORD *your God so as to provoke Him to anger, I call heaven and earth to witness against you today, that* **you shall surely perish quickly from the land** *where you are going over the Jordan to possess it...'*     (Deuteronomy 4:23–26)

Again Moses spoke:

*'If you are not careful to observe all the words of this law which are written in this book, to fear this honored and awesome name, the* LORD *your God, then the* LORD *will bring extraordinary plagues on you and your descendants, even severe and lasting plagues, and miserable and chronic sicknesses. And He will bring back on you all the diseases of Egypt of which you were afraid, and they shall cling to you ... Moreover, the* LORD *will scatter you among all peoples, from one end of the earth to the other end of the earth; and there you shall serve other gods, wood and stone, which you or your fathers have not known. And among those nations you shall find no rest, and there shall be no resting place for the sole of your foot; but there the* LORD *will give you a trembling heart, failing of eyes, and* **despair of soul.***'*
(Deuteronomy 28:58–60, 64–65)

Eight hundred years later the prophet Jeremiah would sound the same trumpet of warning to Judah and Jerusalem, who were about to face their first great dispersion among the nations:

*'... **Why is the land ruined, laid waste like a desert**, so that no one passes through? And the* LORD *said, "Because they have forsaken My law which I set*

*before them, and have not obeyed My voice nor walked according to it, but have walked after the stubbornness of their heart and after the Baals, as their fathers taught them", therefore thus says the LORD of hosts, the God of Israel, "behold, I will feed them, this people, with wormwood and give them poisoned water to drink.* **And I will scatter them among the nations . . .** *"'*
(Jeremiah 9:12–16)

*'And I will give the men who have* **transgressed My covenant,** *who have not fulfilled the words of the covenant which they made before Me, when they cut the calf in two and passed between its parts – the officials of Judah, and the officials of Jerusalem, the court officers, and the priests, and all the people of the land, who passed between the parts of the calf –* **and I will give them into the hand of their enemies** *. . . and I will make the cities of Judah a desolation without inhabitants.'*
(Jeremiah 34:18–20, 22)

Finally, the prophet Ezekiel gives us a poignant picture of the exile and of life beyond the diaspora:

*'Then the word of the LORD came to me saying, Son of man, when the house of Israel was living in their* **own land, they defiled it by their ways** *and their deeds; their way before Me was like the uncleanness of a woman in her impurity. Therefore, I poured out My wrath on them for the blood which they had shed on the land, because they had defiled it with their idols. Also* **I scattered them among the nations, and they were dispersed throughout the lands.** *According to their ways and their deeds I judged them.'*
(Ezekiel 36:16–19)

51

Perhaps I can now outline a few broad tenets based on the Scriptures and as background for the following chapters. First of all, God is in charge of history, and there are no accidents. Next, from the day of Abraham until this present hour, God's highest plans for Israel, and for every person, is that we walk before Him humbly, in godly fear and in quiet obedience. This place of obedience is, by definition, His land for us. If we find Israel scattered among the nations, it is no accident, but by the mighty hand of God, and is the outcome of God's judgments as expressed in His Word. Perhaps half of the entire Old Testament is devoted to the first diaspora, as Israel and Judah were scattered by Assyria and Babylon among the nations. Then follows the precious story of their return. Today, if we still find Israel scattered among the nations, then in the economy of God there is a reason for it.

Paired with the tragedy of the diaspora is the knowledge that God is a merciful God of everlasting love. With the demand for holiness that led to the scattering of the people, He has always a plan for redemption and restoration. Here is the hope for Israel – indeed, the hope for every person who will quietly and humbly return to the Lord in repentance, and to the authority of His eternal Word. The good news of the ages is that the God of the diaspora is the God of *aliyah*! *Aliyah* is God's last great act of redemption. We turn therefore, to *aliyah*: God's last great act of redemption.

# Chapter 6

## Aliyah:
## God's Final Redemptive Act

Before us today is the backdrop canvas of God's call and plan for Israel. A righteous God has called a chosen people to live in a holy manner before Him, and to maintain the holiness of the land into which He led them. Israel was called to be a light to the nations, and to demonstrate to a watching world that a people can serve the eternal God in righteousness and purity. Now the canvas awaits the final painting – of *aliyah*! It is four thousand years since God first cut the covenant with Abram. Twenty-six hundred years since God first had to invoke His ultimate judgment and send Judah and Jerusalem into captivity in Babylon. Nineteen hundred years since the great dispersion of 135 AD under the Romans. And where are those chosen people today? Many are still scattered among the nations of the world.

Is the Lord through with Israel? Sadly, even a majority of the church would vote Yes. Jesus has come, the Son of God among men, and died for the sins of the world. Israel, expecting a messianic deliverer who would re-establish them as prince among the nations, in large part rejected their crucified Lord. In effect, Jesus prophesied as much during His earthly ministry. In an interchange with the Jewish religious leaders, He taught them the parable of the wicked tenant farmers. At the close of that parable, He said:

> '"Did you never read in the Scriptures, The stone which the builders rejected, this became the chief corner stone; this came about from the Lord, and it is marvelous in our eyes? Therefore I say to you, **the kingdom of God will be taken away from you,** and be given to a nation producing the fruit of it. And he who falls on this stone will be broken to pieces; but on whomever it falls, it will scatter him like dust." And when the chief priests and the Pharisees heard His parables, they understood that He was speaking about them.' (Matthew 21:42–45)

How many have seized upon those words: *'The Kingdom of God will be taken from you, and given to a nation producing the fruit of it.'* The conclusion reached seems always to be that God is completely through with Israel; that they will never again have place in His kingdom. However, those who teach this 'replacement theology' – that the church has replaced Israel in God's purposes – and thereby try to excuse themselves from their responsibilities to Israel today, ignore the central principles of God's Word.

First of all, God's ways and His principles never change. Second, when His promises and His covenant say 'forever', then forever is forever. Third, the harshest judgments of the Old Testament prophets were always tempered with the mercies of God: 'If you remember Me in a far land, and if you turn and repent, then I will hear and heal.'

To refute replacement theology comprehensively would go beyond the scope of this book. Yet the pages of the Old Testament prophets are filled with extended passages in which God says, 'I will gather you again to the land'. In every instance, these promises are presaged with the words, 'in the last days', or 'in that day'.

In His third and most mighty act of redemption the Heavenly Father sent His Son, Jesus Christ, to earth to die for our sins and to rise again that we might have life eternal. It was a full and sufficient atonement for all men and all sins and all time. Many argue that the matter is settled and there is no further act of redemption.

In a broad sense this is true. As Paul would put it, no other lamb need die, no other atoning sacrifice need be offered. Jesus was the lamb for all men in every age. Through Him we have Ezekiel's prophesied new heart; through Him we can have clean hearts and renewed minds. Through Him we have life eternal, and through Him we know the fullness of the Holy Spirit.

We might then ask, what is left to discuss? It is finished. But the matter before us is very simple: our heavenly Father is a God of perfect integrity, who lets no promise fall to the ground. And across the pages of the covenant that He cut with Abraham is the mighty stamp of heaven: **FOREVER!** A fourth mighty act of redemption and restoration is in process. I urge on you a systematic study of Romans chapters 9, 10 and 11, where Paul carefully gathers together the vital matter of the place of Israel in these last days. I excerpt briefly a few key points, but follow his argument closely.

> 'For I could wish that I myself were accursed, separated from Christ for the sake of my brethren, my

*kinsmen according to the flesh, who are Israelites, to whom belongs the adoption as sons and the glory and the covenants and the giving of the Law and the temple service and the promises, whose are the fathers, and from whom is the Christ according to the flesh, who is over all, God blessed forever. Amen.'*
(Romans 9:3–5)

*'What shall we say then? That Gentiles, who did not pursue righteousness, attained righteousness, even the righteousness which is by faith; but Israel, pursuing a law of righteousness, did not arrive at that law. Why? Because they did not pursue it by faith, but as though it were by works. They stumbled over the stumbling stone, just as it is written, "Behold, I lay in Zion a stone of stumbling and a rock of offense, and he who believes in Him will not be disappointed." '*
(Romans 9:30–33)

*'Brethren, my heart's desire and my prayer to God for them is for their salvation. For I bear them witness that they have a zeal for God, but not in accordance with knowledge. For not knowing about God's righteousness, and seeking to establish their own, they did not subject themselves to the righteousness of God. For Christ is the end of the law for righteousness to everyone who believes.'* (Romans 10:1–4)

*'I say then, God has not rejected His people, has He? May it never be! For I too am an Israelite, a descendant of Abraham, of the tribe of Benjamin. God has not rejected His people whom He foreknew . . . '*
(Romans 11:1–2)

*'I say then, they did not stumble so as to fall, did they? May it never be! But by their transgression*

56

*salvation has come to the Gentiles, to make them jealous . . . For if their rejection be the reconciliation of the world, what will their acceptance be but life from the dead?'*                    (Romans 11:11–12, 15)

*'For I do not want you, brethren, to be uninformed of this mystery, lest you be wise in your own estimation, that a partial hardening has happened to Israel until the fullness of the Gentiles has come in; and thus all Israel will be saved; just as it is written, "The Deliverer will come from Zion, He will remove ungodliness from Jacob. And this is My covenant with them, when I take away their sins." From the standpoint of the gospel they are enemies for your sake, but from the standpoint of God's choice they are beloved for the sake of the fathers; for the gifts and the calling of God are irrevocable.'*        (Romans 11:25–29)

Paul would gladly have given his own life, like Moses fifteen hundred years before him, for his brethren, who are both sons of the covenant and progenitors in the flesh of the Lord Jesus Christ. Yet, as the apostle to the gentiles, he knows that the nations have come into the kingdom of God before Israel for one simple reason: the Jews would not abandon their works and receive the Messiah by faith. However, Christ is the end of the law for achieving righteousness to those who come by faith.

In crucial emphasis Paul now cries out: has God rejected His people? The answer is clearly, may this never be! Although they stumbled, it was not to be a permanent fall. Rather, it was to give opportunity to the gentile nations to come into salvation. And through this stumbling, a partial hardening has happened to Israel until the time of the gentiles – the fullness of their number – has been accomplished. Then, gloriously, Paul says all Israel shall be saved.

I believe we do not read too much into these three chapters of Romans to say that, **at the very end of the days of this age, the Father's attention shifts back to His chosen family, Israel.** Therefore, rather than the Lord abandoning Israel in these last hours of history, Israel once again becomes the very focus of His gaze; once again the apple of His eye. The question today is: Where is Israel? What is God's plan for her? Now, however, the answer is much clearer. The Lord still loves His people, and His covenant will be restored.

Three times the Father has reached out in redemptive acts which have touched the whole world. In Noah, He found a righteous man and commanded him to build an ark and save His family of eight, while God judged all other men on earth for the evil intent of their hearts. In Abraham, God found a man of faith who would believe Him, and He accounted it to him as righteousness. Through Abraham, we have traced the covenant and family and land, and found the family of Israel to be central to God's plan. He prepared a people to whom He could send His Son. In Jesus, the Father found a servant's heart; the sacrificial lamb who died for the sins of every man in every age.

You may well ask, another redemption? And the answer must be Yes. Not for the sins of the world this time, but for the restoration of His people, His covenant and His land. I pray that in the following pages your heart will leap, as does mine, when you see that God is a God who keeps covenant. Hear Isaiah:

'... *for you will have the* LORD *for an everlasting light, and the days of your mourning will be finished. Then all your people will be righteous; they will possess the land forever, the branch of My planting, the work of My hands, that I may be glorified. The smallest one will become a clan, and the least one a mighty nation. I, the LORD, will hasten it in its time.'*

(Isaiah 60:20–22)

# Chapter 7

# Aliyah:
# God Reclaims the Land

From the earliest days of the covenant God focused on the need for a clean land, where His people could walk out a life of righteousness and fulfill His call for obedience. The reality, however, is that for nearly 2,000 years the land of the covenant has been trampled under the feet of the nations. Since the days of the Bar Kochba rebellion in 135 AD, when Israel fell totally into Roman hands, the land has not known the holy presence of God. Rome turned Jerusalem into a completely pagan city. The land was then held successively by Muslims, Tartars, Mongols, Mamelukes, Ottoman Turks and, finally, the British.

From a spiritual point of view, the land has been anything but clean under her captors for two millennia. From a political point of view, the land identified as Israel in world maps today is but a fraction of the biblical proportions promised by God to the patriarchs. If there is to be a restoration of the covenant, there are four reasons why God must reclaim the land in purity now:

- He Himself must do what Israel as a nation has had neither the faith nor the heart to do: drive out those who are laying false claim to the land.

- If God is to complete the redemption of His people, it must be on a land that is pure, free from the constant evil attacks of the opposing forces of the enemy.

- The land has always been the focal point of the covenant, and if the covenant is to be restored, then the land must be extended to its biblical borders as defined in Scripture.

- The promises of our Lord's return agree that He will return to the same place from which He ascended, as recorded in the book of Acts. That land can hardly be under enemy control. And there is scriptural foundation that the Lord will reclaim His land:

> *'You will also be a crown of beauty in the hand of the LORD, and a royal diadem in the hand of your God. It will no longer be said to you, "Forsaken,"* **nor to your land will it any longer be said, "Desolate"***; but you will be called, "My delight is in her," and your land, "Married";* **for the LORD delights in you, and to Him your land will be married.** *For as a young man marries a virgin, so your sons will marry you; and as the bridegroom rejoices over the bride, so your God will rejoice over you.'* (Isaiah 62:3–5)

Does not your heart leap within you? The land so long called desolate and forsaken is now called married – married to the Lord who delights in her. Even as I write, we can hear the cries of the nations making false claim to the land:

> *'And you, son of man, prophesy to the mountains of Israel and say, "O mountains of Israel, hear the word of the LORD." Thus says the Lord GOD, "Because the enemy has spoken against you, 'Aha!' and, 'The everlasting heights have become our possession.' " '*
>
> (Ezekiel 36:1–2)

Yet in the same prophetic passage we hear the voice of the Lord:

> *'But you, O mountains of Israel, you will put forth your branches and bear your fruit for My people Israel; for they will soon come. For, behold, I am for you, and I will turn to you, and you shall be cultivated and sown. And I will multiply men on you, all the house of Israel, all of it; and the cities will be inhabited, and the waste places will be rebuilt ... Yes, I will cause men – My people Israel – to walk on you and possess you, so that you will become their inheritance and never again bereave them of children.'*
>
> (Ezekiel 36:8–10, 12)

How precious are our Lord's promises in this matter:

> *'For I will take you from the nations, gather you from all the lands, and bring you **into your own land**.'*
>
> (Ezekiel 36:24)

And these further promises:

> *'Thus says the Lord GOD, "On the day that I cleanse you from all your iniquities, I will cause the cities to be*

*inhabited, and the waste places will be rebuilt. And the desolate land will be cultivated instead of being a desolation in the sight of everyone who passed by. And they will say, **this desolate land has become like the garden of Eden;** and the waste, desolate, and ruined cities are fortified and inhabited." Then the nations that are left round about you will know that I, the* Lord, *have rebuilt the ruined places and planted that which was desolate; I, the* Lord, *have spoken and will do it."'* (Ezekiel 36:33–36)

*'When I bring them back from the peoples and gather them from the lands of their enemies, then I shall be sanctified through them in the sight of the many nations. Then they will know that I am the* Lord *their God because I made them go into exile among the nations, and **then gathered them again to their own land;** and I will leave none of them there any longer.'* (Ezekiel 39:27–28)

The desolate land becomes a garden. Ruined cities are rebuilt. The land is once again a choice habitation for Israel. But how can God cleanse the land? As always, He moves through men and nations. For over seven-and-a-half years the Lord has been instructing me in a little discussed end-time war, which I will call the Valley of Jehoshaphat war. Let me briefly outline this war, and show how both its purpose and outcome serve the will of God in cleansing the land. Speaking to the nations, God says:

*'After many days you will be summoned; in the latter years you will come into the land that is restored from the sword, whose inhabitants have been gathered from many nations to the mountains of Israel which*

*had been a continual waste; but its people were*
*brought out from the nations, and they are living*
*securely, all of them.'*                    (Ezekiel 38:8)

The prophet gives clear revelation of the motives of
these nations:

*'Thus says the Lord GOD, "It will come about on that*
*day, that thoughts will come into your mind, and you*
*will devise an evil plan, and you will say, I will go up*
*against the land of unwalled villages. I will go against*
*those who are at rest, that live securely, all of them*
*living without walls, and having no bars or gates, to*
*capture spoil and to seize plunder, to turn your hand*
*against the waste places which are now inhabited, and*
*against the people who are gathered from the nations,*
*who have acquired cattle and goods, who live at the*
*center of the world."'*            (Ezekiel 38:10–12)

The psalmist Asaph gives a parallel picture:

*'O God, do not remain quiet; do not be silent and, O*
*God, do not be still. For behold, Thine enemies make*
*an uproar; and those who hate Thee have exalted*
*themselves. They make shrewd plans against Thy*
*people, and conspire together against Thy treasured*
*ones. They have said,* ***Come, and let us wipe them***
***out as a nation,*** *that the name of Israel be remem-*
*bered no more. For they have conspired together with*
*one mind; against Thee do they make a covenant: The*
*tents of Edom and the Ishmaelites; Moab, and the*
*Hagrites.'*                           (Psalm 83:1–6)

While the nations may believe that it is their idea to
destroy Israel, the Lord makes it abundantly clear that
the war is His:

65

*'And I will turn you about and put hooks into your jaws, and I will bring you out, and all your army, horses and horsemen.'* (Ezekiel 38:4)

Again:

*'And you will come up against My people Israel like a cloud to cover the land. It will come about in the last days that I shall bring you against My land, in order that the nations may know Me when I shall be sanctified through you before their eyes, O Gog.'*
(Ezekiel 38:16)

In a related passage Zechariah speaks for the Lord:

*'Behold, I am going to make Jerusalem a cup that causes reeling to all the peoples around; and when the siege is against Jerusalem, it will also be against Judah. And it will come about in that day that I will make Jerusalem a heavy stone for all the peoples; all who lift it will be severely injured. And all the nations of the earth will be gathered against it.'*
(Zechariah 12:2–3)

The purposes of God in drawing out the nations with a hook in their jaws are most evident. He is bringing them under divine judgment for having scattered His people and for ignoring His glory. Repeatedly, the Lord states that the nations will know that there is a God in heaven, and that Israel too will learn again the majesty of His power:

*'I shall bring you against My land, in order that the nations may know Me when I shall be sanctified through you before their eyes, O Gog.'* (Ezekiel 38:16)

In verse 23:

> *'And I shall magnify Myself, sanctify Myself, and make Myself known in the sight of **many nations; and they will know that I am the** LORD.'*

And again:

> *'And My holy name I shall make known in the midst of My people Israel; and I shall not let My holy name be profaned anymore.* ***And the nations will know that I am the*** LORD, ***the Holy One in Israel.'***
> (Ezekiel 39:7)

> *'And I shall set My glory among the nations; and all the nations will see My judgment which I have executed, and My hand which I have laid on them.* ***And the house of Israel will know that I am the*** LORD ***their God from that day onward.'***
> (Ezekiel 39:21–22)

Couched in the midst of these prophetic passages concerning the Valley of Jephoshaphat war is the clear understanding that the outcome of this battle is wholly in the Lord's hands:

> *'For behold, in those days and at that time, when I restore the fortunes of Judah and Jerusalem,* ***I will gather all the nations, and bring them down to the valley of Jehoshaphat.*** *Then I will enter into judgment with them there on behalf of My people and My inheritance, Israel, whom they have scattered among the nations; and they have divided up My land.'*
> (Joel 3:1–2)

Ezekiel graphically portrays the hand of God reaching into this battle:

> *' "And I shall call for a sword against him on all My mountains," declares the Lord GOD. "Every man's sword will be against his brother. And with pestilence and with blood I shall enter into judgment with him; and **I shall rain on him**, and on his troops, and on the many peoples who are with him, **a torrential rain, with hailstones, fire, and brimstone**. And I shall magnify Myself, sanctify Myself, and make Myself known in the sight of many nations; and they will know that I am the LORD." '* (Ezekiel 38:18–23)

Earthquake, confusion, hailstones, fire and brimstone. But it is the aftermath of this battle that catches our attention. Isaiah says:

> *'Then they shall go forth and look on the corpses of the men who have transgressed against me . . . '*
> (Isaiah 66:24)

In a telling account, Ezekiel portrays these days:

> *' "And it will come about on that day that I shall give Gog a burial ground there in Israel, the valley of those who pass by east of the sea, and it will block off the passers-by. So they will bury Gog there with all his multitude, and they will call it the valley of Hamon-gog. For seven months the house of Israel will be burying them **in order to cleanse the land**. Even all the people of the land will bury them; and it will be to their renown on the day that I glorify Myself," declares the Lord GOD. "And they will set apart men who will constantly pass through the land, burying those who*

68

*were passing through, even those left on the surface of the ground, **in order to cleanse it.** At the end of seven months they will make a search. And as those who pass through the land pass through and anyone sees a man's bone, then he will set up a marker by it until the buriers have buried it in the valley of Hamon-gog. And even the name of the city will be Hamonah. **So they will cleanse the land.'**     (Ezekiel 39:11–16)*

In order to cleanse the land! Three times Ezekiel quotes it. But are they only cleansing the corpses of this most recent battle? I think so, but much more as well. The nations which have camped on the doorstep of Israel for decades and have threatened her constantly with harassment, terrorism and war, trying to drive the Jews out of the land and into the Mediterranean, are now themselves being driven out and destroyed. In fact, further Bible study of the closing hours of history reveals no trace of those nations again.

The premise of this chapter is confirmed: the Lord will reclaim the land and purify it, even to the point where it is married to Him. But just a moment – our study implies that *aliyah* is at the heart of all that is a part of this final redemption. Can it be that the Lord's gathering of His chosen home to the land is playing a significant role in this land-cleansing battle?

And here I stand in awe of the magnificent timing of my Heavenly Father as He ever reveals truth just as we need it. As I write today we are just ten-and-a-half months into the intifada; approximately seventy days since one of the most diabolical terrorist acts in the history of Israel took place. On the evening of June 1, we hear the reports of a suicide bomber who infiltrated the ranks of a large group of young Israelis waiting to enter a disco on the Tel Aviv waterfront. His bomb killed twenty-two young people and wounded scores of others. Instantly in my heart I felt the Father say, 'These young people were *olim* (new immigrants).' Within hours the confirmation came: twenty-one of the twenty-two young people had made *aliyah* from the land of the north. I commented to Carol that not only was this a new chapter in the intifada, but we would soon understand why the enemies of God so hated *aliyah*, the regathering of God's chosen people from the nations.

 Within a few days a young Jewish investigative reporter wrote that the Palestinians in the land had concluded that if they had very large families of twelve to fourteen children, and the Jews continued to have one or two or three children, within two generations – perhaps forty years – they could take the land simply by the electoral process. Yet Israel soon reported that over the last ten years, beginning in 1991, well over one million Jews had made *aliyah*. If the *olim* were immigrating faster than children could be born, then this peaceful battle was lost. Consequently, enormous hatred has developed against the new immigrants.

But did not our God say: *'I will put a hook into your jaw and I will draw you out?'* And could not the sheer numbers making *aliyah* be the very goad which our Lord is using to draw out the nations? What they could not accomplish by the political process must of necessity now be finished by the edge of the sword. In the mighty scope of God's redemptive act, He is very much in the business of reclaiming land, cleansing it, preparing it even as a bride. Zechariah caught the joy of this hour:

> *' "Sing for joy and be glad, O daughter of Zion; for behold I am coming and I will dwell in your midst,"*

*declares the* LORD *... And the* LORD *will possess Judah as His portion in the holy land, and will again choose Jerusalem.'* (Zechariah 2:10, 12)

# Chapter 8

# *Aliyah*:
# God Redeems the Chosen

In the previous chapter I traced God's great inter-vention in the affairs of men for the very purpose of reclaiming the land for Israel. Numerous prophets give a glimpse of this battle in the valley of Jehoshaphat, but Ezekiel gives the fullest account in chapters 38 and 39. As chapter 39 comes to a close, there is a perfect transition from reclaiming the land to the restoration and redemption of both Judah and Israel:

> 'Therefore thus says the Lord GOD, "Now I shall restore the fortunes of Jacob, and have mercy on the whole house of Israel; and I shall be jealous for My holy name. And they shall forget their disgrace and all their treachery which they perpetrated against Me, when they live securely on their own land with no one to make them afraid. **When I bring them back from the peoples** and gather them from the lands of their enemies, then I shall be sanctified through them in the sight of the many nations. Then they will know that I am the LORD their God because I made them go into exile among the nations, and then **gathered**

**them again to their own land;** *and I will leave none of them there any longer.* **And I will not hide My face from them any longer, for I shall have poured out My Spirit on the house of Israel,"** *declares the Lord* GOD.' (Ezekiel 39:25–29)

Here the focus is on God's final act of redemption, first of the land and then of the people. The scripture says that following the cleansing of the land, God will restore the fortunes of Jacob and have mercy on the whole house of Israel (an assurance that He will call back not only Judah, but all of Israel, in this final *aliyah*). Next, the Lord says that they shall live securely on their own land, with no one to make them afraid, and *'I shall be sanctified through them in the sight of many nations'.* Though He has dispersed them into exile among the many nations, He is now gathering them together on their own land and will leave none in the diaspora any longer. In explaining the cause of all this, God says, *'I shall have poured out My Spirit on the house of Israel.'*

It is at once enormously humbling and deeply soul-stirring to be invited by the Father to work in *aliyah*. Yet we need always to keep the scriptural principles straight: it is God who will ultimately gather the Jews back to the land. In the words of Ezekiel, God says clearly: *'I made them to go into exile among the nations,*  *and then I gathered them again to their own land.'* Aliyah is God's agenda, and its ultimate completion is His responsibility. More than seventy times in the Old Testament God says through the prophets, *'I will bring them home.'* Thrilling as it is to participate in some small way in *aliyah*, and to observe prophecy unfolding before one's very eyes, never forget that this is God's holy work.

74

But what do we know of God's purposes? What do we know of His reasons for the regathering of Judah and Israel? Sometimes the Father seems to sense our deep need to understand a matter, and He graciously chooses to spell it out in detail. Happily, this is just such an issue. Before we turn to Ezekiel, let me point out that the following passages are especially welcome because of two different voices abroad that appear intent on twisting the Scriptures. The first, sadly involving much of the church, argues that God is entirely through with Israel – that the church has wholly replaced her – and He will never again turn to redeem Israel. The other, a strident voice, argues vehemently that no Jew has a right to return to the Holy Land until he has first accepted Christ as his Savior. It seems to me that the following passages not only answer both questions, but outline God's plan in masterful detail.

*Replacement Theology*

Ezekiel chapter 36 begins with the enemies of God saying:

> *'Aha! The everlasting heights have become our possession.'*
> (Ezekiel 36:2)

The Lord's response is to speak to the mountains of Israel and say:

> *'Put forth your branches, and bear your fruit for my people Israel; for they will soon come.'*
> (Ezekiel 36:8)

Again in verse 12:

> *'Yes, I will cause men – My people Israel – to walk on you and possess you, so that you will become their inheritance and never again bereave them of children.'*

Turning from the mountains and the land to the people, God then commands Ezekiel:

> *'Therefore, say to the house of Israel, "Thus says the Lord* GOD, *'It is not for your sake, O house of Israel, that I am about to act, but for My holy name, which you have profaned among the nations where you went. And I will vindicate the holiness of My great name which has been profaned among the nations, which you have profaned in their midst. Then the nations will know that I am the* LORD,*' declares the Lord* GOD, *'when I prove Myself holy among you in their sight.'*" '
> (Ezekiel 36:22–23)

In these critical verses is God's highest word on *aliyah*; His clearest, most profound and final warning to the nations that He is God, and great is His Holiness. In His deep love for Israel, the Lord will redeem her – but the message is also a message to the nations that there is indeed a God. Then comes what I believe is the most majestic and transparent statement in the Bible of God's plan for the redemption of Israel:

> *'For I will take you from the nations, gather you from all the lands, and bring you into your own land.* **Then** *I will sprinkle clean water on you, and you will be clean; I will cleanse you from all your filthiness and from all your idols. Moreover, I will give you a new heart and put a new Spirit within you; and I will remove the heart of stone from your flesh and give you a heart of flesh. And I will put My Spirit within you and cause you to walk in My statutes, and you will be careful to observe My ordinances. And you will live in the land that I gave to your forefathers; so you will be My people, and I will be your God. Moreover, I will save you from all your*

*uncleanness; and I will call for the grain and multiply
it, and I will not bring a famine on you.'*
(Ezekiel 36:24–29)

How often the understanding of Scripture hinges on
such simple matters as prepositions, adverbs and
conjunctive adverbs. **For!** For I will take you from
among the nations. Why? So that the nations will
know God's holiness and His majestic glory. **Then!** I
will sprinkle clean water on you. A 'then' indicates that,
given the previous action, the next must follow. Follow
the steps in this passage as God promises them:

> For I will take you from the nations – I will bring
> you into your own land – I will sprinkle clean
> water on you – and you will be clean – I will
> cleanse you from all your filthiness and from all
> your idols – I will give you a new heart – and put a
> new Spirit within you – I will remove the heart
> of stone from your flesh – and give you a heart of
> flesh – and I will put My spirit within you – and
> cause you to walk in my statutes – and you will
> be careful to observe My ordinances – and you
> will live in the land that I gave to your forefathers
> – and you will be my people – and I will be
> your God – and I will save you from all your
> uncleanness.

Perhaps we can now gather a few central principles
about *aliyah* that we have discovered. First, it is not by
accident that Israel finds herself today still largely
scattered among the nations, but in direct response to
the earliest warnings of Moses. Her dispersion nineteen
hundred years ago was a direct consequence of her
strident rejection of the Lord's gift of a Messiah, a

Redeemer. Second, it is the Lord who is now in the process of reclaiming the land for His people and, further, He is providing a holy place to which His Son can return. Third, it is the Lord, who is gathering His people from the far corners of the earth and bringing them back to the land. He has graciously invited many of us to be a part of this glorious process, but He is fully in command. Fourth, only then does the Father promise to sprinkle clean water on Israel, to cleanse her from all filthiness, give her a new heart and put His Spirit within her. Finally, the chief cornerstone, whom Israel rejected in Christ's death and resurrection, will be recognized by the chosen people as their Messiah, the only Son of God. Zechariah describes this time with great poignancy:

 *'And I will pour out on the house of David and on the inhabitants of Jerusalem, the Spirit of grace and of supplication, so that they will look on Me whom they have pierced; and they will mourn for Him, as one mourns for an only son, and they will weep bitterly over Him, like the bitter weeping over a first-born.'*
(Zechariah 12:10)

Fifth, and last, God warns in repeated prophetic revelation that this great process of *aliyah* – although so obviously redeeming the chosen people – is also His last great evangelical gospel to the nations of the world. It is awesome. Thirty-five hundred years later the precious promises of Moses come alive for this day:

*'So it shall be when all of these things have come upon you, the blessing and the curse which I have set before you, and you call them to mind in all nations where the LORD your God has banished you, and you*

*return to the LORD your God and obey Him with all
your heart and soul according to all that I command
you today, you and your sons, then the LORD your God
will restore you from captivity, and have compassion
on you, and will gather you again from all the peoples
where the LORD your God has scattered you. If your
outcasts are at the ends of the earth, from there the
LORD your God will gather you, and from there He will
bring you back. And the LORD your God will bring you
into the land which your fathers possessed, and you
shall possess it; and He will prosper you and multiply
you more than your fathers. Moreover the Lord your
God will circumcise your heart and the heart of
your descendants, to love the LORD your God with
all your heart and with all your soul, in order that you
may live.'*      (Deuteronomy 30:1–6)

Even from the ends of the earth! The Lord will gather
you again and bring you back to the land of your
fathers. Then the promise of a circumcised heart, of a
new love for God that surpasses all understanding – and
of life! God gave the prophet Zephaniah the crowning
word to this majestic vision:

*'But I will leave among you a humble and lowly
people, and they will take refuge in the name of the
LORD. The remnant of Israel will do no wrong and tell
no lies, nor will a deceitful tongue be found in their
mouths; for they shall feed and lie down with no one
to make them tremble.'*      (Zephaniah 3:12–13)

79

# Chapter 9

## Aliyah:
## God Restores the Covenant

How it must have haunted Israel's soul to know that they had broken the eternal covenant cut between their forefathers and the Creator God! All around them were men of lesser scruples and baser morals, who nevertheless faithfully kept human covenants because of the high regard in which such promises had been made. How the cry of the prophets must have been indelibly impressed on their hearts. The Holy Spirit, speaking through the prophets, would recount Israel's great sins before God, but last and most intense was always the lament that they had even broken the covenant of the living God. From the Father's side, there must have been untold grief as He watched His chosen, on whom He had heaped so many blessings, wantonly disregard their commitments to Him.

Throughout Scripture the Lord again and again reminded His people of the integrity of His covenant Word. Isaiah would proclaim:

✓ *'The grass withers, the flower fades, but the word of our God stands forever.'* (Isaiah 40:8)

The psalmist taught his children to sing:

✓ *'Forever, O* LORD, *Thy word is settled in Heaven. Thy faithfulness continues throughout all generations; Thou didst establish the earth, and it stands.'*
(Psalm 119:89–90)

And to a youthful Jeremiah, the Father promised:

✓ *'Then the* LORD *said to me, "You have seen well, for I am watching over My word to perform it."'*
(Jeremiah 1:12)

In a later day Jesus would pledge to His disciples:

✓ *'Heaven and earth will pass away, but My words will not pass away.'* (Luke 21:33)

And Peter wrote:

✓ *'But the word of the Lord abides forever. And this is the word which was preached to you.'*
(1 Peter 1:25)

Today Israel faces a fearsome quandary. The God of Israel has invited, even commanded, her to come back to the land He has restored on her behalf. There He has promised His people a new heart, a new spirit and new life. Yet there hangs between Israel and her God the most awesome rent any garment could ever know; for centuries their forefathers have openly flaunted the Holy Covenant of Heaven. No amount of rigging and fixing, no amount of gerrymandering and patching could ever repair a breach so awesome. Here, bluntly, is the most frightening and hopeless breach in relationships that man has ever known. Desperately sinful man stands accused of covenant breaking before the righteousness of God. Yet this very same God had bid him come – perhaps yet there is hope!

> ' "Nevertheless, I will remember My covenant with you in the days of your youth, and **I will establish an everlasting covenant with you** ... Thus I will establish My covenant with you, and you shall know that I am the LORD in order that you may remember and be ashamed, and never open your mouth anymore because of your humiliation, when I have forgiven you for all that you have done," the Lord GOD declares.'
>
> (Ezekiel 16:60, 62–63)

Jeremiah also expresses this marvelous hope:

> ' "Behold, days are coming," declares the LORD, **"when I will make a new covenant with the house of Israel** and with the house of Judah, not like the covenant which I made with their fathers in the day I took them by the hand to bring them out of the land of Egypt, My covenant which they broke, although I was a husband to them," declares the LORD. "But this is the covenant which I will make with the house of Israel after those days," declares the LORD, "I will put My law within them, and on their heart I will write it; and I will be their God, and they shall be My people. And they shall not teach again, each man his neighbor and each man his brother, saying, 'Know the LORD,' for they shall all know Me, from the least of them to the greatest of them," declares the LORD, "for I will forgive their iniquity, and their sin I will remember no more." '
>
> (Jeremiah 31:31–34)

*'Behold, I will gather them out of all the lands to which I have driven them in My anger, in My wrath, and in great indignation; and I will bring them back to this place and make them dwell in safety. And they shall be My people, and I will be their God; and I will give them one heart and one way, that they may fear Me always, for their own good, and for the good of their children after them. **And I will make an everlasting covenant with them** that I will not turn away from them, to do them good; and I will put the fear of Me in their hearts so that they will not turn away from Me. And I will rejoice over them to do them good, and I will faithfully plant them in this land with all My heart and with all My soul.'*

(Jeremiah 32:37–41)

Jeremiah catches Israel's response:

*' "In those days and at that time,' declares the* LORD, *"the sons of Israel will come, both they and the sons of Judah as well; they will go along weeping as they go, and it will be the* LORD *their God they will seek. They will ask for the way to Zion, turning their faces in its direction; they will come **that they may join themselves to the*** LORD **in an everlasting covenant that will not be forgotten.'***

(Jeremiah 50:4–5)

Finally, Ezekiel reveals very clearly the connection between the reclamation of the land and the restoration of the covenant:

*'And they shall live on the land that I gave to Jacob My servant, in which your fathers lived; and they will live on it, they, and their sons, and their sons' sons, forever; and David My servant shall be their prince*

*forever. **And I will make a covenant of peace with them**; it will be an everlasting covenant with them. And I will place them and multiply them, and will set My sanctuary in their midst forever. My dwelling place also will be with them; and I will be their God, and they will be My people.'*      (Ezekiel 37:25–27)

That's it! A new covenant, an everlasting covenant of peace. Yet note!

*'From the very beginning the Lord God saw that the wickedness of man was very great on the earth, that every intent of the thoughts of his heart was only evil continually...'*      (Genesis 6:5)

Therefore the new and eternal covenant which the Lord showed both Jeremiah and Ezekiel must of necessity require a new heart for man. Now the central premise of this book can be summarized: it is through *aliyah*  that our Lord achieves His last great act of redemption – even the restoration of a covenant long-broken. Let Ezekiel describe this sequence beginning with *aliyah*.

*'Therefore say, Thus says the Lord GOD, "I shall gather you from the peoples and assemble you out of the countries among which you have been scattered, and I shall give you the land of Israel." When they come there, they will remove all its detestable things and all its abominations from it. And I shall give them one heart, and shall put a new spirit within them. And I shall take the heart of stone out of their flesh and give them a heart of flesh, that they may walk in My statutes and keep My ordinances, and do them. Then they will be My people, and I shall be their God.'*
(Ezekiel 11:17–20)

We are finally coming to the complete redemption of Israel. First, God gathers them from among the nations. Then, He gives them the new land. They remove all the 'detestable things' and cleanse the land. Next, He gives them a new heart, taking away the heart of stone and giving them a heart of flesh. Now they are able to walk in God's statutes and keep His commandments. At last they can be His people, and He can be their God.

To the unredeemed heart there remains one staggering question: How can the righteous God write a new covenant with me, a sinful man? How can He remove the dead heart of stone, and replace it with a living, vibrant heart of life? Praise God! Jesus answered that question on the night before His crucifixion:

> *'And in the same way He took the cup after they had eaten, saying, "This cup which is poured out for you is* **the new covenant in My blood."'**      (Luke: 22:20)

It is here that the returning *olim* meet their Savior and Lord – our Savior and Lord – Jesus Christ. The new covenant is restored as the Father, in fulfillment of His promise, removes the stony heart, and replaces it with the redeemed heart of flesh. He cuts a new covenant through the blood of Jesus! The apostle Paul gathers all these matters together succinctly, and writes of Jesus:

> *'But now He has obtained a more excellent ministry, by as much as He is also the mediator of a* **better covenant**, *which has been enacted on better promises. For if that first covenant had been faultless, there would have been no occasion sought for a second. For finding fault with them, He says, "Behold, days are coming, says the Lord, when I will effect a new*

*covenant with the house of Israel and with the house of Judah.*'' (Hebrews 8:6–8)

*'But when Christ appeared as a high priest of the good things to come, He entered through the greater and more perfect tabernacle, not made with hands, that is to say, not of this creation; and not through the blood of goats and calves, but through His own blood, He entered the holy place once for all, having obtained eternal redemption. For if the blood of goats and bulls and the ashes of a heifer sprinkling those who have been defiled, sanctify for the cleansing of the flesh, how much more will the blood of Christ, who through the eternal Spirit offered Himself without blemish to God, cleanse your conscience from dead works to serve the living God? And for this reason **He is the**  **mediator of a new covenant,** in order that since a death has taken place for the redemption of the transgressions that were committed under the first covenant, those who have been called may receive the promise of the eternal inheritance.*(Hebrews 9:11–15)

And therein, my friends, is the hope of *aliyah* reflected in a restored covenant. The dead heart of stone which kept Israel in rebellion for centuries is now replaced with the heart of flesh. The shed blood of our Savior Jesus, so much better than the blood of bulls and goats, now atones for the sins of all Israel, and enables them to walk in love and obedience before their holy God. Jesus then is the mediator of the new covenant! And *aliyah* brought them back to face reconciliation in their long estrangement from the living God.

# Chapter 10

# *Aliyah*:
# God's Refining Fire

Our picture is nearly complete. *Aliyah*, the regathering of God's chosen people from the farthest corners of the earth, is the great fulcrum around which He is orchestrating these final moments of history. As Israel streams back to the land in large numbers, God has used *aliyah* to provoke the nations into confrontation over the increasing number of settlements in disputed territory. Eventually the land will be reclaimed, and Israel will blossom as prophesied.

As we shall see, this gives the Lord an opportunity to wash His people in clean water, and put His Holy Spirit upon them. He will redeem them through the new covenant, which He Himself is now restoring. This covenant was always focused on the land and God's purposes for His people, and God's last great act of redemption is being worked out as He gathers His people home.

The Lord impressed on me one final message as I waited before Him: all that He is working out on behalf of His covenant in Israel is at the same time His last great evangel and witnesses to the nations – and to us.

When Paul described these last hours, he warned that they could not come until the apostasy, the great falling away, had come first:

> *'Let no one in any way deceive you, for it will not come unless the apostasy comes first, and the man of lawlessness is revealed, the son of destruction.'*
> (2 Thessalonians 2:3)

An objective assessment of our society must confirm that this apostasy is upon us. Yet God will leave no man without a witness. Again and again throughout the scriptures prophesying *aliyah*, the Lord concludes by saying, 'And then the nations will know that there is a God in heaven.' Psalm 83 vividly portrays the nations conspiring to wipe Israel off the face of the earth, and concludes:

> *'Let them be ashamed and dismayed forever; and let them be humiliated and perish, That they may know that Thou alone, whose name is the* Lord, *art the Most High over all the earth.'*
> (Psalm 83:17–18)

The prophet Joel saw God's last witness and His judgment on the nations bound up in one act:

> *'For behold, in those days and at that time, when I restore the fortunes of Judah and Jerusalem, I will gather all the nations, and bring them down to the valley of Jehoshaphat. **Then I will enter into judgment with them there** on behalf of My people and My inheritance, Israel, whom they have scattered among the nations; and they have divided up My land.'*
> (Joel 3:1–2)

In Ezekiel's comprehensive portrayal of the last hours of history, the Holy Spirit repeatedly brings us back to this central theme:

*'My dwelling place also will be with them; and I will be their God, and they will be My people. **And the nations will know that I am the** LORD **who sanctifies Israel**, when My sanctuary is in their midst forever.'* (Ezekiel 37:27–28)

Ezekiel is speaking to Gog and the ten-nation conspiracy as he writes:

*'And you will come up against My people Israel like a cloud to cover the land. It will come about in the last days that I shall bring you against My land, in order **that the nations may know Me** when I shall be sanctified through you before their eyes, O Gog.'* (Ezekiel 38:16)

That same chapter closes with:

*'And I shall magnify Myself, sanctify Myself, and make Myself known **in the sight of many nations; and they will know that I am the** LORD.'* (Ezekiel 38:23)

Put very simply, *aliyah* is God's last great refining fire for the nations. In some instances He will gather them right up to the city of Jerusalem, and there judge them with fire and brimstone. Yet to men and nations everywhere, *aliyah* is **God's last powerful witness that He is God**, and is **in control of history**. Think of it! A nation that has not existed for two thousand years is suddenly re-established, even as a Prince among nations. A people who have been scattered among the nations to the farthest corners of the earth, and should have been assimilated within two generations, are now, two thousand years later, being called back to that land from the most remote villages, caves and forests. The words of Micah come alive:

> *'I will make the lame a remnant, and the outcasts a strong nation, and the LORD will reign over them in Mount Zion from now on and forever.'* (Micah 4:7)

As the Lord restores the covenant and redeems Israel, His very acts are a burning witness to the nations, a refining fire.

The final question is: What should *aliyah* mean to us? Many of you who pick up this book will already have a great love for Israel deep in your hearts. Some will have felt the mighty touch of His call, and know a specific plan of how He would have you work in the vineyard of *aliyah*. It is a prophetic and scripturally founded call:

> *'And He will lift up a standard for the nations, and will assemble the banished ones of Israel, and will gather the dispersed of Judah from the four corners of the earth.'* (Isaiah 11:12)

> *'When the LORD will have compassion on Jacob, and again choose Israel, and settle them in their own land, then strangers will join them and attach themselves to the house of Jacob. And the peoples [goyim, gentiles] will take them along and bring them to their place.'* (Isaiah 14:1–2)

> *'Thus says the Lord GOD, "Behold, I will lift up My hand to the nations, and set up My standard to*

> *the peoples; and they will bring your sons in their bosom, and your daughters will be carried on their shoulders."'* (Isaiah 49:22)

What an awesome and holy calling to be invited by our heavenly Father to help gather His chosen people home. God said that to touch Israel was to touch the apple of His eye, but I sense that even more fearsome would be to force one's own agenda on God's ingathering: it would be to tamper with His holy plan. Perhaps no other work in God's kingdom requires such great caution. We need to carefully hear and heed His will and to avoid casual involvement.

*[handwritten margin note: Caution!]*

When David longed to bring the ark back to Jerusalem, the men were casually carrying it on a new cart drawn by oxen, rather than on poles on the shoulders of the Levites as specified in Scripture. At one point the oxen nearly upset the cart, and a man called Uzza reached out to 'help God' by steadying the ark on the cart. This careless disobedience, although well-intentioned, incurred God's wrath and Uzza was consumed on the spot. *[handwritten mark: ✗]*

Just as the Lord is using *aliyah* to reclaim His land, redeem His people and restore the eternal covenant, so I would urge on any who are under divine appointment to work in *aliyah* that this truly is a redemptive work. My personal testimony is that the closer I come day by day to *aliyah*, the more I sense God's refining fire in my own soul. All who are touched by *aliyah* will find it to be the refiner's fire, drawing us closer to His holiness and purity.

> *'"Sing for joy and be glad, O daughter of Zion; for behold I am coming and I will dwell in your midst,"*

*declares the* LORD *...And the* LORD *will possess Judah as His portion in the holy land, and will again choose Jerusalem."'* (Zechariah 2:10, 12)

If you have enjoyed this book and would like to help us to send a copy of it and many other titles to needy pastors in the **Third World**, please write for further information or send your gift to:

**Sovereign World Trust**
**PO Box 777, Tonbridge**
**Kent TN11 0ZS**
**United Kingdom**

or to the **'Sovereign World'** distributor in your country.

Visit our website at **www.sovereign-world.org**
for a full range of Sovereign World books.

Ebenezer Emergency Fund
P.O. Box 26
Point Harbor, NC 27964
Ph. 252-491-9201
E-mail: eefusa@juno.com
www.ebenezerusa.com